HOW TO TRANSFORM YOUR BORED PUP INTO A CONTENTED DOG

Easy Ways To Entertain Your Bored Dog When Walks Are Limited

By

Becky Oldfield

CONTENTS

<u>Introduction</u>

Firstly, thanks for picking up this book and well done for making your dog a top priority. I know there is always so much else to think (and worry) about but they will be very grateful that you have taken the time to think of them and try to make the situation better for them too.

There could be any number of reasons that you are unable to walk your dog as much. Maybe you are unable to walk far yourself, maybe your dog is recovering from an injury or surgery themselves or you might simply be very busy!

For me, it is that I am restricted from walking my dogs as much as they are used to. At the time of writing this in the UK we are currently still under various restrictions, which prevent us from leaving our homes much and it is such a tough time for everyone but not least our dogs. I hope you are doing ok. I'm sure you're feeling the same as me - worried, frightened, anxious and confused. It feels like everything we thought we knew is now wrong and we find ourselves having to adapt to this new worrying reality.

I really do know how hard it is at the moment; after all we're all in the same boat to some extent. But we can try to look at some of the positives in this awful situation. One is that most of us now seem to have more time at home than perhaps we've ever had before. And you know who IS going to be happy about that change? That's right, our dogs! Cherry, my working cocker spaniel is delighted (Finnegan my dachshund not quite so much, I think I'm getting under his feet!).

Your dogs are the most loyal creatures you will ever meet and they love us more than anything. What's more - they don't care about the situation because they don't understand

what is going on.

We can take a huge amount of strength and comfort from them during this awful time and we can try and use this extra time with them to really develop a fantastic bond with them as friends and team mates, not just pets. They will also need more from us as they are having to adapt to these huge changes too.

It is highly likely that, just like my dogs, your pups are having to make do with less exercise than they were previously getting. Or maybe you are now limited as to where you can walk them. At the time of writing this we are still allowed out to exercise but only once a day. Lots of us are combining that with the need to walk our dogs but it may be less than they are used to. On top of that, for many dogs, their entire routine has changed. Maybe you are now working from home, or furloughed, and maybe the kids are now home too.

While your dog will no doubt be delighted to be spending so much time with you all, it is still a huge change for them, and they may be finding it hard to adjust. Can you imagine spending most of your day chilling at home in peace, snoozing on the sofa and waiting for the family to come home to suddenly being in a busy house, full of people and noise 24/7? I reckon it would come as a bit of a shock to me too!

So, with this in mind, and knowing that we are a bit limited at the moment, in this book we will focus on some simple things that you and your dog can do together to keep each other happy and fulfilled.

Before we go any further, I'll just do a quick introduction (not too long though I promise). My name is Becky Oldfield and I live in a little village called Collingbourne Kingston in Wiltshire with my husband, our two dogs, Finnegan an eleven year old miniature longhaired dachshund and Cherry a three year old working cocker spaniel, as well as five chickens.

I run a professional dog walking business, but we don't actually offer bog-standard walks; instead we run adventures. These are much more structured than a normal walk but also much more fun. They are packed full of activities, games, mental stimulation and training. I have two amazing ladies who work for me: Ruth and Helen. Ruth has been with me over three years now and the dogs all adore her. Helen was about to start just before all this kicked off (isn't that sods law) but we're looking forward to her joining us. I also have my "staff" not on the payroll – Cherry & Finnegan....

We are unfortunately, closed temporarily at the moment and I am missing all the dogs like mad. They are

like family to me; lots I have been walking for many years and some I have known since their mums and dads first brought them home at 8 weeks old so have such a bond with them. I know I'll see them again but, in the meantime, I've been busy trying to come up with lots of activities and games to keep them occupied and happy.

If you want some tips outside of this book on things you can do to keep your pup entertained, I have a free resource for you as a thank you for buying this book. Simply head on over to our website and fill in your details on this page www.contenteddogs.co.uk/bored-dog-free-guide I will send you the link to a webinar I did a few weeks ago on some simple ways that you can use food to entertain your dog.

So, let's get cracking!

Chapter 1 - Keeping Your Dog Safe

I know, I know, this isn't the fun games and tips that I promised! But hang in there, we will get to them, but this bit is important too.

On or Off Lead?

Firstly, now more than ever, we need to make sure that we keep our dogs close by when out on walks. If your dog has a fantastic recall, or rarely wanders far from you, that's brilliant and will be extremely useful during these strange times. You might still want to keep on top of practising the recall lots or train them to an even better standard. Why not set yourself a mini challenge and see how quickly they can come to recall?

If, however, your dog has been known to "turn rogue" and head for the hills after that rabbit, wander out of sight following that really interesting scent, or absolutely insist on just saying a quick hello to that stranger and their dog then you might consider keeping them on lead on walks for now. This need not be the end of all freedom for your dog; you could use a long line instead of your normal lead as these still allow your dog a good amount of freedom but importantly you are still in control.

If your dog were to become lost at the moment, people may not be able to help you search for them and it would increase the risk for all involved, including the dog warden.

Secondly, and this applies all the time, your dog always needs to be wearing a collar and tag. The Control of Dogs Order 1992 states that every dog in a public place must wear a collar and/or a tag at all times which includes the owners name and address. Telephone number is optional but personally I include it as I would want my dogs to be back with me as soon as possible and anything I can do to speed that up I would! You do not have to include the dog's name, and indeed some believe you should leave that off in case it makes it easier for dog thieves. That bit is down to personal preference though. There are some exceptions to this law, such as working dogs or packs of hounds, but in general it applies to all.

In this respect, now is also a good time to just check that your pup's microchip details are up to date. You would be surprised how many dogs are found who are chipped, but the owner's details are out of date or incorrect. I've almost forgotten to update my own dogs' microchip details before. You know what it's like when you move to a new house, there are a million things to do and this is one that is very often forgotten. Depending on the microchip company, you can usually amend your details online or over the phone.

Keep Your Distance

Keeping a certain distance from others is another thing to be aware of. I'm sure you are all well up to speed with how far to stay away from other people by now; it's even marked out for us in the supermarkets. (How weird is that by the way?!). But your dog does not understand the new normal and has no idea that they are meant to stay two metres away from that neighbour or postman that they always say hello to.

At the time of writing this, there is no evidence that dogs can contract or transmit the infection, but it has been said that they may be able to transmit it briefly on their fur. I'm most definitely not a scientist so I have no idea whether this is true or not, but to be on the safe side I would avoid letting people outside your household stroke your dog and don't let your dog approach them. This is easy for Finnegan who is a bit of a wuss with strangers but the social butterfly that is Cherry is finding this a bit of a challenge. I almost had to rugby tackle her the other day to stop her harassing the DPD driver as she was so desperate to see someone other than us after all these weeks!

Heat

This next one might seem a bit over the top, especially for us in the UK where we mostly just have rain followed by drizzle - followed by more rain, but the heat is something to be aware of.

I'm sure, like me, when you are all at work and it's hot you have made sure the area of the house your dog is kept in is cool and well ventilated and they have access to fresh water. It may sound silly but when you are at home all the time it is easy to forget this. Finnegan is a real sun-seeker and if we leave the back door open and he has free access to the garden, he will literally lay in the sun all day until he roasts and I have to physically bring him inside when I think he's getting too hot.

Heatstroke is a big risk for dogs. They are very susceptible to the heat. Unlike us, they can't sweat through their skin, instead they lose heat mostly through panting but also through sweat glands in their pads. Symptoms of heatstroke include excessive panting, drooling, reddened gums, loss of coordination and collapse, among others.

Keep your dog cool by avoiding walking during the hottest times of the day and always have clean drinking water available. Watch your dog closely on your walk for any signs of agitation or overheating. If you think your dog may have heatstroke move them to a cool shaded area immediately and use cool (not freezing) water to wet their coat and contact your vet. Most vets are still taking emergency cases even if they are closed for non-essential visits and they will be able to give you more advice over the phone or through an online consultation. Also avoid walking on pavements when it is hot as dogs' pads can be easily burnt. Sunburn can also be a problem for some dogs, especially those with short or light-coloured coats.

Right, now we've got the less interesting stuff out of the way let's move on to the best bit, the fun things you can do with your dog.

The main activities this book is going to cover are mental stimulation (or brain games if you prefer), tricks and preparing your dog for being left alone again. All of these are based on trying to provide your bored pup with activities that will tire them out, keep them happy and content and make your life a little easier in the process.

<u>Chapter 2 - Mental Stimulation</u>

You have probably heard this term a lot in relation to your dogs (and my clients will be able to testify that I'm always banging on about it!) but might wonder what the big deal is. You walk them, feed them and love them, but is there more you could be doing to make sure your precious pups are truly content? For such amazing and complex creatures, dogs have fairly simple needs, but we do need to fulfil them and it need not be as complicated as you think.

This is even more important if their physical exercise may have been reduced. But worry not! You might be surprised just how tired your dog is after ten to fifteen minutes of mental stimulation.

All dogs need, among other things, some form of challenge in their lives, something to stimulate those wonderful brains of theirs. Mental stimulation has so many benefits for our dogs. For a start it reduces stress levels in the dog. Depending on what exercises you are doing, some can increase your dog's mobility and fitness. It enhances their memory. Similarly, the process of learning new things keeps their minds active and healthy as well as boosting their confidence.

But it's not only our dogs who benefit, you probably already know this but it's actually really fun to do things with your dog and spending quality time together like this and really concentrating on doing something that they need is immensely rewarding and strengthens the bond between you too.

Unfortunately, boredom in our dogs is incredibly common with more and more dogs being given up for rehoming due to various behavioural problems; many of which originate from the fact that the dogs are not getting the exercise and stimulation that they need.

Luckily, there are a whole host of things you can do - most of them at home, and as an extra bonus they won't take long and are super easy too.

Use the Food!

Finnegan lives for food. He never used to be that greedy until he was about five and the vet told us that he was a little bit overweight and could do with losing maybe half a kilogram. You can imagine how mortified I was. I had let my dog get fat, what a dreadful owner! He's only little too so it shows more on him, though I tell him he's big boned, so his feelings aren't hurt. So anyway, I dutifully put him on a diet (he actually ended up losing about a kilogram in the end so my bad again) but ever since then he turned into the greediest dog around. I don't know if he's worrying that I might suddenly stick him on a diet again or what it is, but he will do literally anything for food.

He cannot be trusted with it either, once we accidentally dropped a big chunk of cheese on the floor, and I mean big, and he immediately snatched this prize. In his haste to stop us taking it from him he swallowed it whole and began to choke, I could literally see the chunk of cheese-sized lump in his throat - it was terrifying! He did bring it up again after a second or two just as we leapt into action, but it felt like hours. Anyway, this just shows how much of a valuable resource food is for dogs, especially cheese in Finnegan's case....

A lot of these games are based on using food, but it is such a fantastic tool to use, most of us don't use it enough with our dogs. We just plonk their meals down once or twice a day, depending on how often they are fed, and let them get on with it. I must admit I'm often guilty of doing this too. But we can use it in so many ways and your dog will enjoy it even more, I promise.

You might be wondering what food you should use for these games. Well it does not always have to be treats; why not use your dog's daily food allowance but instead of putting it all in their bowl at dinner time, save some of it for using in these games. You can of course use treats too, or healthy snacks like chopped up carrots or apples (not the core or pips though as these are toxic to dogs and consult your vet first if your dog is diabetic as they have a high sugar content). I tend to do a bit of both.

While we are on the subject there is a fun little test you can do with your pup to find out which are their favourite treats. First prepare a selection of treats - say for example, kibble, hot dog chunks, cheese, ham, carrots, shop bought treats and so on.

Then choose two and hold one of each in each hand and make a fist. Offer the closed hands to your dogs and let them sniff both, then gradually move your hands away. Your dog will follow one rather than the other. Repeat just to be sure. Then take the next two and do exactly the same. Continue with the other treats and you can gradually narrow it down to which are your dog's absolute favourites, and which less so.

This is useful because you then know which are the highest value to your dog and it is these that you would use for the harder things, like if you are training outside where there are lots of distractions. The less high value could then be used for at home; saving the amazing ones for when you need them most! You might be surprised; I've walked some dogs who have turned their nose up at cheese but loved boring old biscuits!

You might also be wondering how much food you should be using for these games. It does not have to be loads. Indeed, you might want to be a bit mindful of how much they are eating, especially at the moment if their exercise has had to be reduced a bit. Being overweight brings all sorts of problems in itself.

My dachshund Finnegan is a bit like me, he's only got to look at food and he puts on weight, so I have to be careful with him (and he is so greedy!). You can also break treats up into really small pieces, for lots of dogs it's not the size of the treat but the fact that they are getting one at all. My boy for example, thinks chewing is not really for him - he just shovels it down anyway so the size is really irrelevant.

If you're worried about overfeeding you can also reduce the size of their main meals a little to accommodate this, although try not to replace too much of their meals with treats as their main food is likely to be complete foods and contain all the nutrients your dog needs so we don't want them missing out on too many of those.

There are lots of reasons that food is a great thing to use to keep your dog happy and entertained. For a start most dogs love food! And don't worry if your dog is not usually a foodie, for these try the really exciting treats, a bit of cooked liver perhaps or warm cooked chicken. If they still aren't interested, you can replace food in some of these games for toys.

It is also a very natural behaviour for dogs to work for their food rather than just being given it. Obviously, our pups aren't wild animals, but they are descended from them and if they were in the wild they would have to hunt for their own food.

Using food is a brilliant and really easy way to add in the all-important mental stimulation to your dog's day, with some of these you will hardly have to think about it. This is surprisingly tiring for dogs so is a great way to add in some exercise for them. This is a lifesaver for me now with Cherry.

When I'm at work she normally comes on most, if not all of the adventures so she's used to a good few hours a day of physical exercise - though being a working cocker, she would happily do double this. She is getting nowhere near this now sadly, but these games are more than making up for it.

Dogs also love a challenge; they love to use their brains. Using food in the ways that I will show you gives them loads of opportunity to do this and you will be able to see for yourself how much they enjoy it. It is an easy way for you to add this into their day and it is all simple things, nothing you will have to sit down and learn and think about.

Using food in this way also comes with the added bonus that it can make your dog's mealtimes last a bit longer. Finnegan lives for food (they do say you're like your dogs don't they!) and if I just give him his meals in a bowl they last literally seconds but if I use them in some of the ways I'm going to tell you about it means he can enjoy them that bit longer, which is always a good thing in his eyes.

Lots of these games are also great for relieving stress in your dog. Many of them will be encouraging your pup to use their nose more and sniffing is incredibly calming for dogs. In fact, one study found that the actual act of sniffing was more rewarding for the dog that the finding itself.

Let's move on to the games.

<u>Chapter 3 - Six Searching Games</u>

Cherry and Finnegan love searching games. It's hard to imagine at the moment with all the lovely weather we've had but in the deepest darkest depths of winter a couple of months ago, I was out on one of the work adventures and like an idiot must have dropped my glove somewhere. You might not think this is the end of the world, but it was minus two and I was ten minutes in to a ninety-minute adventure. What a disaster! Luckily I had super sniffer Cherry with me though. I asked her to find the glove and off she went (If I'm honest I wasn't holding out much hope, sometimes she's very clever but at other times not the brightest bless her!). You can imagine my deep joy when she reappeared with the rogue glove. No frozen fingers and chilblains for me! She is a pro at these searching games by now though; they really encourage and help your dog to use their nose. Don't forget too, how stress-relieving and calming sniffing is for dogs.

1. *<u>Find It</u>*

We will start with a nice easy one, what I like to call the "find it game" (I know, very original!). This game can be played in several ways and is really simple to do. Both of mine love this game and I do too; it's one of the games they can both play at the same time too and really useful if you have more than one dog.

The first is essentially scatter feeding. You take a handful of whatever food you are using, maybe their normal food, or treats broken up into little pieces and then sprinkle it on the floor. You can play this game in the house, in the garden, or even out on the walk. We quite often add a few "find it" games into our adventures at work and the gang love it. If your dog has not played this before, start off by making it really easy for them and if needed, help them to find the food by showing them where it is. Encourage them by telling them to "find it".

By the way, it won't take your dog long to learn that phrase. On the adventures, if I say who's ready for a "find it" game, I suddenly have several very attentive pups sat at my feet gazing up at me!

A slight variation on this game is, instead of sprinkling the food, you keep the dog in another room while you hide the treats in various places around the room (or garden). Then let your pup back in and ask them to find it. Again, start off really easy and put the treats in very obvious places, or use especially smelly treats which will help the dog.

As they get better at it, they will gain confidence and you can then make it a bit harder, maybe make the hiding places less obvious or out of sight altogether. Keep a close eye on your dog though, if they look like they are struggling or losing interest give them a hand as it has to be fun for them.

Another way to play the "find it" game is by splitting your dog's meal into several portions in different bowls and then hiding those bowls around the house. Just like before encourage them to find it and give them loads of praise when they do. Help them too if they are struggling, they will soon get the hang of it. It is worth bearing in mind if you have more than one dog you might want to take it in turns and shut one in another room while you play the game with the other. If I did this with my two at the same time, I can guarantee Cherry wouldn't eat as Finnegan is like a heat-seeking missile with this one!

If your dog is getting super clever at this one, why not make it even more of a challenge for them by putting their meal in a Kong or other similar food dispensing toy so that when they find it they have the added fun of trying to get the food out of it.

You might be able to come up with some variations on this yourself. Have a think and more importantly have a go - your dog will be happy either way as they will have you interacting with them and they will love getting their noses working.

1. *Finding Toys*

You don't have to limit yourself to only using food for the "find it" game; you can also use toys too. I tend to save the toy finding games for out on our walks, but you can play them in the house in exactly the same ways as you do with the food.

Before starting this game, it is useful to try to determine which toys your dog prefers over others just like we did before when we worked out which treats were really high value for your dog and which perhaps less so.

If you have a good idea already of what your dog's favourite toys are then you are onto a good start. If not, spend a few minutes down on the floor with your dogs playing with them, with various toys. Using two or three at a time, see which one your dog chooses over the others. You should be able to spot which ones they prefer. Repeat this, narrowing it down until you have several favourites.

You don't necessarily need to spend the earth on toys. You may find your dog prefers an old toilet tube or empty plastic bottle to that expensive super tough toy! These are the ones to take out on your walks with you as you want your dog to think you are the best and most interesting thing on the walk, not other dogs in the distance and not that squirrel they have just spotted.

Playing the find it game with toys on your walk is really good fun, I think I enjoy it as much as the dogs! Basically, it involves hiding toys in the environment you are in and asking your dog to search for them. I use a similar cue as with food. "Find the ball" (or toy), sometimes adding in a bit of encouragement such as "where's the toy/ball etc..." but if you want to use a different one that's absolutely fine too.

Just like before, if your dog is new to this game make it easy to start with and then gradually make it harder as they get the hang of it. I would even start by just placing the toy a few feet in front of them where they can see it and asking them to find it.

When they do this make a huge fuss of them and tell them how clever they are, gradually increase the difficulty and hide the toys out of sight and ask your dog to find them. You can use any toys for this, but it makes life easier for you if you use their all-time favourite toys as they will be much more motivated to find them. For Cherry, the tennis ball is the ultimate toy, but Finnegan cannot be bothered with toys outside of the house; it's food only. Apparently, toys are for indoor use only. He has some strange life rules bless him - but who am I to argue?

If there are two of you on the walk, it can make it a bit easier to play this game as one of you can stay with your dog on lead while the other hides the toys. Then you can release your pup to search for them.

Don't worry if you are on your own, you can still play this game easily. On the work adventures we don't walk together - and Michael (my husband), is still at work at the moment, so I often walk my two alone at home too. If your dog is especially good at 'stay' and will happily stay when asked while you hide the toys that's great. If not, and don't worry because lots of dogs can't resist moving from a stay when something exciting like this is happening, I have a couple of tricks I'll share with you. I have gotten quite good at this as when walking up to six dogs there is always someone watching me lol, which makes it hard to sneakily hide toys without them seeing!

If you only have one dog, you can gently cover their eyes with your hand and quickly throw the toy. You can then ask them to find it straight away or mix it up by walking with them a bit further away and then asking them.

With more than one dog, this would obviously be a bit harder, but I have a little tip for this too. If you are a master of stealth, simply keep walking and act nonchalant, then dawdle a little and when your dogs are ahead of you discreetly drop or throw the toy off to the side. The aim is for the dogs not to see where the toy is so that they get the fun of hunting for it. If your dogs are wise to your tricks (all the work gang know me now and keep an eye on me most of the time!), you can also make a big show of throwing one toy away from you, then when they are heading off after that throw another quickly in a different direction. It sounds simple but trust me it works.

I love this game and it is a really popular one on our adventures too. It is perfect for when walks are limited too as this will tire your dog out so much more than simply walking as they will be so much more engaged as well as using their brains and noses too.

2. *Box Search*

When Finnegan was a puppy all those years ago we used to give him old boxes to play with (he had loads of toys too - I'm no Scrooge) and he used to love tearing them up, flinging them around and investigating them. If you have never seen a miniature dachshund puppy tearing around dragging a cardboard box twice his size you're missing out! He still loves them to this day. If we get parcels delivered, he follows us around waiting for the box which he thinks he is entitled to....

Empty cardboard boxes or finished toilet roll tubes (assuming you've actually managed to buy toilet paper in the first place in the current madness), are great tools to create some fun activities for your pooch - so start saving them. Don't worry, this is super-simple though.

Just make sure before you start that the box is safe and does not have anything on or in that your dog could hurt themselves on and they are not going to get their heads stuck in. Also supervise them when playing these games to make sure they do not eat any cardboard or anything else that they shouldn't.

Just like with the previous games, you can use treats or your dog's usual meals for this. And again, if at any time they seem to be struggling, help them out and make it a bit easier for them. Start with one box, put some treats in it and encourage your dog to find it. If they played the 'find it' from before they should be experts at this now. That should be nice and easy as they will be able to see the food. Then do the same again but this time put some scrunched-up paper or other, smaller, boxes in too.

If you don't have any don't worry - you can also use towels or blankets rumpled up; it has the same effect. Again, ask your dog to find it. It will be a bit harder this time as they are having to use that wonderful sniffer of theirs instead of their eyes!

Now they have the hang of this you can start adding multiple boxes and doing the same thing with each of them. Start off by putting treats in all of the boxes but as they get better at the game, just put it in some of them, rather than all so that they have to work that little bit harder to find the food. Then let your dog search them all and give them loads of praise when they find the ones containing the prize.

This is a great game for adding mental stimulation as it really gets their noses going and it's great to get them problem-solving, especially if you use a variety of different box shapes and sizes as they will have to really think and work out how to get the food out of each one. It is also so easy and most of us have at least one or two empty boxes hanging around waiting for the recycling.

3. *Tea Towel Treasure*

The tea towel treasure game is a personal favourite of mine. Friday nights for us are sacred. I know every day feels like a Friday at the minute for some of us but humour me for a bit. Anyway, Friday nights we try our best to not make any plans at all. Our usual work week is pretty manic, so we like to keep that night free for… wait for it… pyjamas, a film and a bottle of wine. (If we're lucky some Pringles too). Exciting, right?! I know it's boring, but I really look forward to these nights. It's just lovely to have time to relax and not have to think about anything and lose myself in a film.

But you can guarantee that Finnegan and Cherry will get bored and want to play. I don't know about yours but as soon as they've had their dinner, they seem to go mad raiding the toy box, tearing around the living room and generally haranguing us to join in. I often make a couple of these up ready for them as they really enjoy them, and they keep them occupied for a surprisingly long time.

For this game you won't need much, and I'd be surprised if you didn't already have the bits in your house now. You just need, for each dog, treats (or part of their daily food allowance), two empty toilet roll tubes and a tea towel.

Start by folding the tea towel in half. Then sprinkle some treats over the towel. Starting at the edge, roll the tea towel lengthways tightly, rolling towards the treats until you have a sausage shaped roll. Then slide a toilet roll tube onto each end and pull along so there is a few centimetres of material on the outside of it. Depending on how tightly you rolled the towel, you might need to wedge it in. You should end up with a long sausage shape with a cardboard toilet roll on each end. Voila!

Did Anyone Mention Sausages?

Give this to your pup and watch them have fun working out how to get to the yummy treats that they can smell inside!

You can change this game slightly if you don't have any empty toilet rolls. Just take a tea towel, or any piece of material of a similar size. Place treats on it as mentioned above. Then take the two opposite corners and tie in a very loose knot. Do the same with the other two corners and give to your dog to work out.

Just like the others, it is best to supervise your dog with this one as we don't want them eating cardboard or tea towels! You can make this game easier by rolling the towel loosely and harder by rolling it more tightly. This one is a great game for dogs who are normally speedy with puzzle games as it should be a little bit harder for them. This is a firm favourite with my two - hope yours enjoy it too.

4. *The Cup Game*

Have you ever heard of something called the shell game? It is very old; in fact it's thought to date back to ancient Greece. It is a gambling game but one that was often actually a con. A ball is hidden under one of three identical cups or other containers. Whoever is operating the game then shuffles these around quickly and people can place bets on which cup the ball is underneath. It is commonly used by con men though who actually rig the game by hiding the ball while they are shuffling the cups around.

Does She Know I'm Colour-Blind?

Don't worry, we're not going to turn our dogs into tricksters - but we are going to do something very similar for our next game, which is a very fun one.

For this you will need treats and three identical containers that the dog cannot see through, such as plastic cups, egg cups, pots and so on. It doesn't really matter what you use, but just check that they are safe for your dog and that they are not going to break if they knock them over. With your dog watching, place all three cups face down on the floor and hide a treat under one of them. Ask them to wait and, with your dog watching you, slide the cups around several times with the bottom of them not leaving the floor. They should now be in a different order than before. Then ask your dog which cup the food is under.

This is quite a fun trick too as with lots of practise it looks like your dog is watching and remembering which cup is the one that is hiding the treat, when in reality it is their noses that they are using again. You can play this game in different ways, depending on how hard you want to make it for your dog.

To start with, let them knock the pot over to get the treat underneath but to make it a little harder why not teach them to indicate which pot it is with their nose or paw for you to then hand them the treat. Have a go with your dog, it's a fun way to spend some time with them.

5. *Treat Dispensing Toys*

I'm sure you have heard of a Kong before. How about a snuffle mat? Or a lickimat? There are hundreds of dog toys like these on the market now; you probably have one or two kicking around at home but how often do you use it? These are fantastic tools for adding in some really easy mental stimulation and fun for your dogs if you're stuck at home, with the added bonus that it hardly requires any effort at all. They also involve your dog searching or using their nose and brains to find the food. Kongs are brilliant and may be the best well-known of them all. You can get them in various sizes and various levels of toughness which is great for the chewers! You can put almost anything in a Kong, they are just so versatile.

If you haven't got one already, they are easy to pick up online. You can just use them to feed your dog's normal meal in if you wish. We feed our two on raw food, so I quite often stuff their meal into the Kong for them to eat it that way as they have to work a bit harder for their food, which they really enjoy. I will sometimes also add a smidge of peanut butter (make sure it does not contain xylitol, an artificial sweetener added to some peanut butters, as this is highly toxic to dogs) or cheese spread on the top so that they feel they're getting something special! You can stuff any variety of treats in that you can think of really.

Kongs can also be frozen, which is a great treat for a warm day but also takes the dog much longer to get the food out. Sometimes I will also hide the actual filled Kong itself and send them to find it, so they get two games in one, a searching game followed by the fun of working out how to get the food out - they love it. Why not try hiding a filled Kong in a box like we did with the treats earlier? There are loads of other similar toys on the market too and we have quite few in this house.

Another great tool to make the most of during this time is a lickimat. These also come in a huge variety, including a wobble version which is shaped like a bowl and, like the name suggests, wobbles as the dog is using it. These work really well for raw food but are also great for keeping your pups entertained in general. They lend themselves really well to spreadable treats like cream cheese or peanut butter (no xylitol remember!). Licking itself is very calming for a dog too so they are great for keeping our pups calm and happy during this stressful time especially if they are picking up on our stress and worry.

Another great toy to get your dog using their nose is a snuffle mat. You can either make these yourself or buy them. I bought mine as I am rubbish at things like that, but they are definitely worth it. They are usually a square or round piece of plastic mesh with lots of pieces of felt threaded through. You can sprinkle and hide treats in this and give it a ruffle with your hand so that the treats work their way in. Then your dog has to "snuffle" their way in and search for the food; loads of fun for them and another great bit of mental stimulation.

Don't worry if you haven't got any of these though, and if you don't want to splash the cash at the moment, there are some DIY versions you can have a go at. Just be sure to always supervise your dog, especially if it is one you've made yourself and check that there is nothing that the dog can hurt themselves on and no small pieces that they could swallow.

A good alternative to a snuffle mat is just some old towels or blankets all scrunched-up together with treats hidden in the folds. Your dog will have a great time trying to sniff out all the goodies.

You can also have a go at making your own treat-dispensing toy by using things like cardboard boxes or empty plastic milk cartons (give them a wash first). With cardboard boxes you could cut a few holes in and then pop some treats in and seal the box back up.

Let your dog work out how to get the food out.Similarly, empty plastic milk cartons are great fun; some dogs love plastic bottles anyway - Cherry certainly does, but if they contain food too how much more exciting are they then! Leave the lid off the bottle and cut some holes in the sides.

To make it easier for the dog make the holes larger and to make it harder cut them smaller. My two love this one and spend ages bashing them around the room so that the treats fall out. So that's our six searching games to play with your dog to keep them occupied and happy. You could probably add to this list yourself so why not have a think of others you could try.

Chapter 4 - Six Fun Tricks to Try

All dogs are clever, in fact some are more intelligent than we might think! Michael was home alone with Finnegan one night while I was out. He had treated himself to a Dominos that night (this was when we still lived in range for delivery, not out in the sticks where nowhere delivers like now). He thought he would have a relaxing night enjoying his pizza and a beer in front of the TV, but he failed to take the 'Finnegan factor' into account.

He told me Finnegan was hanging around hoping for a taste of Texas BBQ pizza but then disappeared. Then the moment he had a beer in one hand, a slice of pizza in the other and the rest on his lap, Finnegan appeared from nowhere, made a huge leap in the air (bearing in mind he's a dachshund so has very short stumpy legs), grabbed an entire slice of pizza from the box and shot off behind the sofa with it!

He has never done that before or since; in fact he usually has incredibly good manners while we're eating, so I have no idea what got into him. I thought it was hilarious - I mean it wasn't my pizza, but also the fact that he must have assessed the situation, planned his strategy with military precision and made his move at just the right time really amused me.

Pizza-Boy

Finnegan is a dog that always needs a challenge; he's very intelligent and absolutely loves learning. Dachshunds are a working breed originally so are very bright, though he has never worked a day in his life! Despite this he still needs to be kept busy and training is a great way to do this and keep him out of mischief at the same time.

If you are at home more, now is a perfect time to brush up on your pup's basic training but why not add in some fun stuff too as well as the usual suspects like heel, recall, stay etc. Why not have a go at some tricks? Dogs love learning and if it is something new you will really get their brains working. My two dogs love all forms of training.

I only have to say the word "training" and they get excited but if it is something new, they really do switch on and I love seeing them so happy and engaged. Learning a new trick really tires them out too, which is so useful at the moment as we are so limited on how much we can do so why not give their brains a workout as well as your one walk a day. I have not met a dog yet either who doesn't enjoy learning something new.

It also strengthens the bond between you, which is such a lovely feeling. You probably already know this anyway so even more reason to have a go at some of these. It also increases your dog's confidence. The more they learn and the more successful they are, the more their confidence increases when trying new things. This is wonderful to watch too, especially with dogs that are not generally very confident.

Training tricks are also just really fun. There's so much going on at the minute and most of it is pretty awful so it's nice to add something positive in that you and your dog can both enjoy and take your mind off the news for a while. The world is your oyster with tricks, you may be surprised what you can teach your dogs to do, from a basic sit right through to putting the washing in the machine for you and anything and everything in between.

First lets just concentrate on six simple tricks that you can start with, that will get you having some fun with your dog:

1. *Spin*

Spin is a great one to start us off with. It is pretty straightforward too so no need to spend hours swatting up on dog-training books. I think most of the dogs that come on our adventures know this one now and they love it. On a good day I can get them to spin one at a time - but mostly I say "spin" and they all go at once; not quite as polished but great fun!

To teach spin we use something called "luring" which is actually pretty easy to get the hang of. You take a treat and show it to the dog, then holding the food just in front of their nose you move it slowly and use it to guide them into the position you're aiming for, then lots of praise and give them the treat. You can also use toys for this instead of treats. Say, for example, you wanted to teach your dog to sit. You would take the treat or toy, hold it in front of the dog's nose and gradually move it up and above the dog's head. As they follow it, they will naturally move back, and their bum will go to the floor. You praise at that moment and give them the reward.

It is very similar with the spin. Hold the treat in front of your dog's nose and very slowly guide your dog around so that they are moving in a clockwise circle. Then lots of praise and give them the reward.

You can start off by rewarding any small movements heading that way, for example quarter or half turns. Then gradually build it up until they are following your hand with the treat in for a full clockwise circle. Keep your hand low at the dog's nose level for now so that they are not tempted to jump up to get the treat.

Once they are doing this consistently you can add in your cue; I use "spin", but you can call it whatever you like. As they get better at this you can bring you hand up higher and eventually you won't need to lure them at all.

If you have got the hang of this, why not have a go at teaching them to spin the other way, anti-clockwise. I use "around" for this but again you can call it whatever you prefer. You do this in the same way as above but this time going in the opposite direction.

One tip though is do not try to teach your dog both spin and around at the same time as you may end up with a confused pooch who isn't sure what way they should be going! Try teaching them one direction first until they are good at that and then start on the other.

2. *Hand Touch*

I love this one. This is teaching your dog to touch the palm of your hand with their nose when you ask them to. It sounds really simple but it's such a useful trick to have up your sleeve, you never know when you might need it. You can use it to redirect your dog away from something else or simply to get their attention back onto you.

You can also build on it to form all kinds of other behaviours or tricks. I used this to get Finnegan to touch various named objects and then built on that to teach him to push a door open or closed. You can use it to improve your heel work or use it as the basis of getting your dog to retrieve something to your hand; it is great and so versatile.

Start off by placing a small treat in between your fingers and with your hand open show your palm to your dog. They are likely to move forward to sniff it and the moment their nose touches your hand say "yes" or "good" or whatever you usually say to mark when they have done it right. Then give them the treat from that hand. Repeat this several times, each time praising your dog when they touch your hand with their nose and giving them the treat that was between your fingers.

Once they are touching your hand consistently, do the same again, but this time without the treat placed between your fingers. Just like before, as soon as they touch your hand with their nose, mark it with your "yes" or "good" and give them a treat.

Keep practising this and once they are consistently touching your hand with their nose every time you show them the hand, then you can add in your cue word. I use "touch".

Now practise asking your dog to "touch" and showing them your hand. They should be happily bopping your palm with their nose then looking to you for their reward.

When you're starting off try to keep your hand in roughly the same place each time but once they know the trick you can start moving your hand around to make it a bit harder for them and get them thinking a bit more. Try putting your hand in different positions, at different heights or moving the hand around so that your dog follows it. If they are struggling with anything at all just go back a step and practise the stage that you were doing before until they fully understand what you want.

You can leave this one as it is if you like but there is another way that you can make the hand touch trick a bit harder and use it to tire your pup out a bit more. If you are stuck at home or maybe can't walk them as far or as long as normal then this is a great way to take the edge off the excess energy they may have as it is both mentally and physically tiring. It is also pretty fun for them!

This time, we do the same as before and ask your dog to touch your hand but this time when they do, instead of giving the treat to them, you are going to throw it a short distance away so that they have to run to get it. As your dog eats the treat and turns around to look at you, show them your hand again so that they run back to touch it, then throw another treat. Start with throwing the treat a fairly short distance - just a couple of feet, we want the dog to be able to see it, but then gradually increase the distance that you are throwing it.

You should end up with a very happy dog racing out to get the treat that you have thrown before hurtling back to touch your hand and repeat the process. Ten minutes of this can be surprisingly tiring for them!

If you want to go a bit further with this one, why not teach your dog to touch various objects. If they know the hand touch you can build on this to ask them to touch other items, such as toys or bits of furniture, whatever you like really. Learning the names of objects like this and differentiating between them really does get their minds working.

You can do this by using your hand and pointing at the object while saying touch and rewarding them first for any movement towards the item but after a while only rewarding them when they actually touch it, then finally adding the name of the item. But there is a handy little trick I use, post it notes.

Start with a few normal hand touches. Then take a sticky post it note and put it in the same hand and ask your dog to "touch". They will usually touch the post it note as they try to touch your hand. Repeat this until they have the hang of it. Now you can place a post it note on something else, say a door for example, and ask the dog to "touch" and point at the post it note. Stay quite close to the item to start with, as they get more confident at this you can move further away.

Once your dog is consistently touching the post it note with their nose, start adding in the name of the item before your touch command, so for a door it would be "door touch". Keep practising and after a while you can fade out the touch part of the cue and just say "door".

Again, with more practise you won't need the post it note either, that is just a target to help your dog while learning this. You can then extend this and teach your dog to touch other named objects. Finally when they know several names of items ask them to touch one by name and let them work out which one it is. Take your time with this though as it's very mentally tiring but great stimulation for them.

3. Through

Our third easy trick is "through". This involves you standing with your legs slightly apart and your dog running under your legs when asked. It is another easy but fun one that you and your pup can do together.

Start off by standing with your legs far enough apart that your dog could comfortably walk through them underneath you. Then take a treat and drop it on the floor between your feet. Show the dog if they have not seen it. Repeat this step several times.

Then start dropping the treat a bit further back, just a little bit to start with, but gently throw it through your legs so that it is just behind you. Your dog should go under your legs to get the treat. Again, gradually increase the distance that you are throwing the treat so that your dog is starting to go a bit further to get it.

Once they are starting to get the hang of this start adding your cue word "through" just before throwing the treat under your legs. After a few repetitions of this stop actually throwing the treat but still mimic the action of throwing it under and when they do go through give them a treat by hand.

After practise, you should be able to say "through" and do the hand gesture for throwing a treat and your dog will run through your legs then look at you expectantly for their treat.

1. Figure of Eight

This is a really fun one, and once you've got the hang of it, it looks pretty cool too! With this one, you will be able to say "figure of eight" and your dog will weave through your legs in a figure of eight motion while you're standing. Imagine a number eight on its side, that's the shape we're trying to get your dog to do but going through and around your legs to do it.

Just like with the spin, I use luring for this trick. Stand with your legs far enough apart that your dog can comfortably move through them. Take a treat and hold it near your dog's nose, then very slowly lure them into the first part of the eight; through your legs, around the back of your left leg, around to the front and then back through your legs again, but this time going around the back of your right leg then ending up in front of you. Make sense?

Start off very slowly with this one as it can be a little confusing for the dog at first. It is also sometimes easier to start off teaching them one half of the eight, just going through and around your left leg, then move on to teach them the second half, around the back of your right leg. As they get more confident with it you can go a little faster, but still using the treat to lure them, until they are consistently following the treat and making the figure of eight movement. Then start adding your word.

I use "figure of eight" but you can call it whatever you like. With some practise, you will no longer need to lure them and when you say your cue word and are standing with your legs apart, they will do the figure of eight through your legs.

If you have got the hang of that and wanted to take it a step further, you could turn it into a *leg weave,* where your dog weaves through your legs as you're walking. Cherry doesn't know this one as I haven't taught her yet, but Finnegan does. I have to walk a bit slowly as he's old and not the speediest, but he loves it.

This is really similar to the figure of eight, but this time have your dog at your side when you start rather than in front of you. Then take one big step forward and hold that position while you use a treat to lure your dog under and around the outside of the leg that you have stepped forward with. Give them lots of praise and the treat. Then take an exaggerated step forward with the opposite leg and do exactly the same but on that side instead.

Repeat with the other leg again and then the other one again and so on. Remember to give your dog loads of praise and a treat for each leg they go under to start with. As they get better at this you can wait until they have weaved through both legs before giving the reward and then gradually extend the amount of steps and weaves they do before you give them their treat. Just like before, once they have the hang of it you can start giving them the cue word "weave" just before they start the action. Have fun!

2. *Paws Up*

Most of our adventure dogs know this one. It is good fun and you can do this anywhere, both at home and out on walks, and on almost anything. At home I tend to use the coffee table, a chair or my arm but out on a walk trees or logs are a good option. Your dog will be able to jump up and rest their front paws on whatever you are pointing at.

This is another trick that you can use luring for, and you are probably well up to speed with that by now! Start off teaching your dog this trick at home. I use our coffee table for this as it is quite low and both Finnegan and Cherry can easily reach it.

Just a quick note though: if you have a big dog, or indeed any dog that you may not want jumping up on the furniture just teach them on things you are happy with them putting paws up on, avoid the dinner table! You can also use a sturdy box or similar.

Say, for example, you are using the coffee table. Start off sitting on the floor with your dog and some treats. Hold the treat in front of your dog's nose and lure them by moving the treat up and slightly over the table. As they follow it, they should jump up and put their front paws on the table to get closer to the treat. Reward them then and give them lots of praise. Repeat this action several times and once they are getting quicker at putting their front paws up on the table start to add in the cue "paws up" just before they do the action. After a few repetitions they should be able to carry out the action when you say "paws up".

Now they know the trick you can start practising it on other objects or on your arm, if your dog is small enough or your arm is strong enough! Do exactly the same while holding your arm out horizontally and asking your dog to "paws up". Your dog should get the hang of this faster as they already know the trick now. If they don't, just lure them up into position like you did before. Practise on lots of different objects or when out on your walks you can use trees or logs and so on. If nothing else, it makes for some very cute photos!

There are some little add-ons you can do with this trick if you want to. One I particularly like is "say your prayers". This is easier to do if your dog is doing the paws up on your arm. Ask them for "paws up" with your arm held out. When they place their paws on your arm take another treat and, holding it close to your dog's nose, very slowly move it downwards so that they follow the direction of the treat with their nose.

They may jump off your arm and if they do simply repeat but make the action of moving the treat down a bit slower this time. At first reward them for any little downward movement of their head but gradually increase the distance they have to look down before giving them the treat. Practise lots until your dog is following the treat down with their head but keeping their paws up on your arm.

You can also teach a "move round" while in the paws up position. This one is best done if they are using a table or log, or anything else that they have room to move along. When they are in the paws up position, use a treat held just above them and use it to lure them along the object so that they are shuffling sideways with their paws still on the object. Make sure to do this one very slowly though!

The Things I do For Love....

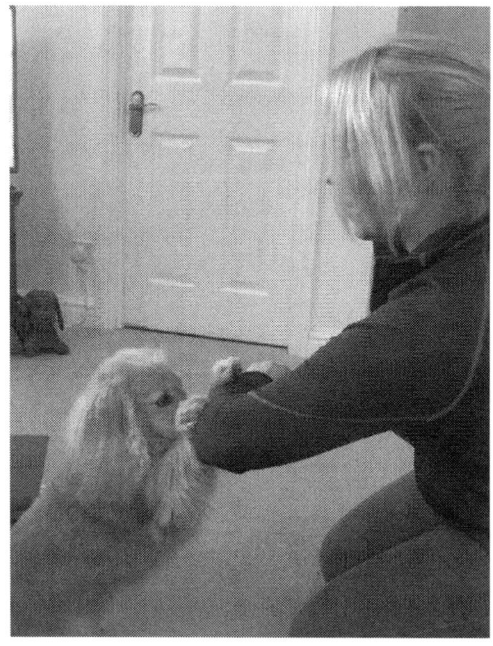

3. _Reverse_

I taught Cherry this one as she is very enthusiastic about toys and gets so close waiting for me to throw it, she is almost climbing up me! I wanted to be able to ask her to move back a bit but can't use the word "back" as I use that for certain retrieves that she does. So, I called this one "reverse" but you can pick any word you like as long as you're consistent with it. The aim with this one is to get your dog to move backwards away from you. Make sure you have some tasty treats to hand.

Cherry is a sensitive soul

I started this one with me kneeling on the floor so that I wasn't looming over the top of her but if your dog is bigger or less sensitive you can stand too, whatever is more comfortable for you.

Start moving very slowly towards your dog. As you get closer and closer, they will move back a little. It might be as subtle as shifting their weight back at first rather than physically moving. That's fine - reward that and give them lots of praise.

Keep repeating this until your dog is starting to physically move back a little bit when you move towards them. Make sure you reward any backwards movement at first, no matter how small. Gradually you can build this up until you only reward the bigger backwards movements. Keep practising this but over time you should be able to reduce how close you get to your dog before they back up a bit. Once you only have to move towards your dog a small step or two and they are moving backwards start adding in your cue "reverse" just before they move.

Try to remember to smile too. Sometimes when I'm concentrating, I frown and you don't want your dog to think you're moving towards them looking cross about something!

So those are our six simple tricks to teach your pup and I hope you like them. If anything is unclear please do feel free to join our Facebook group, which contains videos of all of these. I will give you the link in the last chapter.

<u>Chapter 5 - Preparing Your Pup For Being Left Alone</u>

I am sure, like me, you will be so pleased when we are able to get back to some kind of normality, even if it is different to before. We are living in such uncertain times; I think we will just have to wait and see what happens. But even if it happens gradually, we will get back to some kind of normal at some point and we need to remember that our pups might feel very differently about it than us.

I know we are all in different situations; some of you may be still working the same hours as before, but some may have been home all the time for weeks on end now. For those of us who have been at home much more than normal, we need to start to prepare our dogs for the changes to come. For one thing, they will have become accustomed to us being at home with them much more than normal, maybe even constantly. If we suddenly go back to being away all day again, it is highly likely they are going to struggle to adjust to this huge change.

Separation anxiety is very common and is extremely upsetting, both for our dogs and for us too. But there are some things we can do to try and prepare our pups and avoid them going through unnecessary stress. We can start to introduce some short periods of time where your pup is left alone so that they do not become reliant on you being with them all the time. I know this is easier said than done at the moment with such restrictions on our movements, but it can be done.

You may still be going out at some point, even if it is just for essential journeys such as getting the shopping. If you live alone, in this respect it is a bonus as your dog has a set period of time alone fairly regularly.

You can and should also factor in periods of time at home

where your dog is separated from you all. Try shutting them in a separate room, maybe with a Kong or suitable chew toy to keep them occupied, while you go about your business. Try to do this for short periods several times a day. It may not feel nice not letting them be with you all of the time but you really will be doing them a favour and setting them up for success when we do all go back to work and school.

Whether your dog usually has the run of the house or is left in a certain room while you are out, why not take a coffee and a book and sit in your car on your drive for an hour or so while leaving them in their usual area. It may sound silly, but it is still preparing your dog to be left alone again.

Gradually increase the time they are left and start off with short periods and slowly extend it. If your dog is already showing signs of separation anxiety such as howling, going to the toilet in the house, or being destructive, this gives you time to contact a behaviourist who will be able to help you to help your dog. Many are still offering online consultations.

If you can, it would also be helpful to stick to as much of a routine as you can. For example, try to stick to roughly the same feeding and walking times as you usually do if possible. Dogs are creatures of habit and if they are already in a similar routine to what we are going to expect them to do we will help them immensely.

<u>Chapter 6 – Conclusion</u>

I really hope you have found this book at least a little useful and hope it helps you to not only keep your pup happy and entertained, but also to start thinking about how they will cope when we start to get back to work and school.

This is a first for me and is easily the most I have written since University, which is a very long time ago now so please excuse any mistakes! I don't know if you're like me and are worrying about your dogs not getting enough attention at the moment but rest assured you are doing a brilliant job. They will cope, they will get to the other side of this. The fact that you have made the effort to read this to get some ideas on things to make their lives better means you're already a great dog mum or dad and they are lucky to have you.

If you want to learn more, please head on over to my website www.contenteddogs.co.uk Why not join our mailing list? I will send you the link to the webinar on some simple ways that you can use food to entertain your dog. Simply got to my website and fill in your details on this page www.contenteddogs.co.uk/bored-dog-free-guide

We would love to see you in our Facebook group too, there are videos of all the games and tricks mentioned in this book, plus lots more if you want to try others. Simply search for Contented Dogs on Facebook.

If you've enjoyed this book, please send me an email at becky@contenteddogs.co.uk and if you're feeling especially kind, could you please leave me a review - I would be very grateful!

Take care and stay safe,

Becky x

About the Author

Becky Oldfield is a professional dog walker, who lives in a small village called Collingbourne Kingston in Wiltshire along with her husband Michael, miniature dachshund Finnegan, working cocker spaniel Cherry and five very

demanding chickens.

She runs Contented Dogs, a premium dog adventure business specialising in activity and games-based walks for dogs, which was founded in 2010.

When not working, she can usually be found walking or training her own dogs and failing that, sat on her backside watching TV with a glass of wine....

www.contenteddogs.co.uk

Acknowledgements

I just wanted to say thank you to a few people who have helped me lots, especially during this difficult time.

Firstly, thank you Michael for helping me so much, bringing me lots of coffee and walking the dogs for me while I was writing, I love you lots.

Thanks to my mum Molly, brothers Josh and Dan, and mum and dad in law, Heather and Chris, love you all lots. Hopefully we will be able to see each other properly soon.

I'm so grateful too to Terri and Mitch, who very kindly took so much time and proof-read, edited and formatted the photos for this book, you were brilliant and I really appreciate it.

My mentor Dom Hodgson has been amazing too, he has made my little business so much better and more fun than it ever was before and has inspired me to keep on improving it, cheers Dom!

A big thank you to my amazing staff, Ruth, Helen and Emma (who sadly left recently but will always be an honorary part of the team!), thanks so much for sticking by me, hopefully we will be back out again soon.

Thanks so much to all my wonderful friends and clients (lots of you are both!) I really appreciate your loyalty and support through all of this, I cannot wait to be back out on adventures with your pups again soon!

x

Printed in Great Britain
by Amazon

56459127R00031